CONTENT IN THE DIGITAL AGE

ANITA JOSEPH

Content in the Digital Age
Anita Joseph

First published in India by TDW
All Rights Reserved.
©2022

Published by
TDW Productions & Publishing

ISBN: 978-93-91828-10-3

Type Setting & Design
TDW Digital Graphics
thedigitalwordhub@gmail.com
Web: www. http://tdwpublishing.com/

CONTENT IN THE DIGITAL AGE

ANITA JOSEPH

TDW Productions & Publishing

TDW Productions & Publishing
www. http://tdwpublishing.com/

Disclaimer:
The publisher or editor shall not be held liable for any factual errors or misrepresentation by any of the authors in this book. The responsibility for opinions expressed in articles or contributions rests solely with the author/individual authors and publication does not constitute an endorsement.

CONTENTS

PREFACE 9

1 THE 'DIGITAL-FIRST' MINDSET 12

2 WHY THIS FUSS ABOUT CONTENT? 16

THE STORY - 1 RADIANT CANDLES 19

THE STORY - 2 AMBER's CUPCAKES 23

3 WRITING vs STRATEGY 28
vs MARKETING

Profile-ONE   Ruchika Nagpal Mehta 31
Founder, Patavya Diamonds

4 INVESTING IN DIGITAL CONTENT 34

5 WHY MARKET CONTENT? 37

6 GETTING IT RIGHT 40

Profile -`2 Gunjandeep Singh 44
Founder, Aroma Souls

7 THE DOs & DON'Ts 46

8 CONQUERING THE 49
CONTENT FEAR

Profile 3 Debabrata Mandal 52
Founder, DM India

9 PRINT vs DIGITAL 55

10 SOCIAL MEDIA PLATFORMS 58
& CONTENT

11 THE IMPORTANCE OF 62
STRATEGY

Profile- 4 Vighnesh Jha 65
Director, Hum Shilpakar

12 KNOWING YOUR AUDIENCE 67

13 CUSTOMER EXPERIENCE MAP 70

14 SEO-THE KEY TO GETTING FOUND 73

15 VIDEO CONTENT-THE BEST WAY TO TELL YOUR STORY 77

Box:1 YouTube Driving the 'Creator Economy' *83*

16 SOCIAL MEDIA CONTENT 85

Box:2 TikTok Creator Fund *89*

Profile-5 Varalika Mishra 90
Founder, Your story is Important

17 VLOGGING vs BLOGGING: WHICH IS BETTER? 93

18 PODCASTS-IN OR OUT? 99

Box: 3 Podcast Market *103*

Proflie- 6	*Deepak Nair* *Entrepreneur and Digital* *Media Pioneer*	104
19	OTT PLATFORMS: DRIVING THE CHANGE	109
20	CONTENT CREATION ON OTT PLATFORMS	112
21	ANALYSING CONTENT	114
Proflie-7	*Harpreet Ahluwalia* *Founder & CEO, Earthly Creations*	117
22	CAN TRADITIONAL CONTENT CREATION METHODS SURVIVE?	120
23	CAN I USE CONTENT TO MAKE MONEY ONLINE?	123
24	DISPELLING SOME MYTHS	128
25	TO SUM IT ALL UP	131

PREFACE

"If you want to be influential, diversify your portfolio by elevating your content across digital platforms building your brand by focusing on innovation, fan engagement and audience development."

— *Germany Kent*

The world of digital content has exploded upon all of us and no one is immune from its effect. To attempt a journey into a landscape that is so complex and complicated at the same time, is a task fraught with difficulty and uncertainty.

There's one thing, though: the digital world is not for the faint-hearted-it is for the bold, the insanely creative, the unabashed risk-taker. So, if you're willing to put yourself out there, shout out loud and carve a niche, then digital is for you. If you're an entrepreneur or a startup looking for better reach and traction, then yes, digital is the way to go. If not, stay away!

I was a newbie to the digital world until my innate curiosity forced me out of my complacency. From thinking that print was the final word in content, to thinking that a website was the be-all and end-all of the digital world, I've come a long way. And during my journey, I've discovered the pleasures of the digital world-the freedom it provides and the unlimited number of takes and retakes it permits. Now I'm hooked-and I know I can only go further on this road of discovery.

The idea for this book came about when I decided to consolidate my penny-worth of thoughts on the subject for others like me who're navigating the digital landscape. Mistake it not for a pedantic outpouring of familiar gabble - all I aim to do is deconstruct the digital content creation world with those who would like to know.

Then again, my attempt in this book is not to unravel the digital content realm in its entirety-that would be futile and frustrating, to say the least. Rather, my effort is to touch the tip of the iceberg-to understand and help understand the basic concepts and terms that define this unique landscape.

The digital ecosystem is still evolving, and so many of these terms are inter-related and inter-connected. I've not embarked on them in great detail-only just touched upon what I think is important for a digital traveller like me who loves to explore and discover.

I have also attempted to answer as many questions as possible that digital content creators often face-for instance-how can I ensure maximum reach for my brand with the digital content that I create? Will I be able to make money? Is content writing the same as content marketing?

My answers are by no means exhaustive. This is only an attempt to provide some perspective and clear some of the fog surrounding them.

The aim of this book is to inform and be informed-there are concepts and terminologies I have used here that have taken on greater dimensions and become a lot clearer even as I write this-so I hope my readers will excuse any and every incompletely explained, "grey" area(s) for this very reason. It's my fervent prayer that I'll learn from this book as much as I hope to enlighten my readers with it.

Anita Joseph
January 2022

1

THE 'DIGITAL-FIRST' MINDSET

*The first step to digital transformation is from
the baseline-cultivating a digital-first mindset.
This takes effort, but it's worth it.*

Change is always hard. Especially when it involves a complete overhaul of thought processes and daily operations, this change can be excruciatingly painful. Sometimes, this change can be so complicated, that the transition becomes slow and gradual. Take the case of the digital, for instance. The whole shift from the physical has been so monumental, that even today, businesses and individuals that have been forced to make this change, are struggling to adapt.

I remember, for instance, when YouTube arrived, many found it difficult to subscribe to channels that they liked to watch, simply because they thought that hitting the subscribe button would mean paying money! Today this has changed, but the fear of the digital unknown still persists. However, digital transformation is an inevitable process and if you haven't begun it already, you're likely to fall out of the reckoning really quick. Content is an part of this transformation. It represents the face of the digital world - this is where its potential and possibilities are concretised.

This is the first question that plagues anyone who desires to move with the times-how and where do I begin?

Like everything else, the first step to digital transformation is from the baseline-cultivating a digital-first mindset. This takes effort, but it's worth it. The aim should be to bridge the divide between generations-the older set who have been completely in-ured to the physical and the newer lot who have been born into the digital. Awareness is key here and it's absolutely crucial to let everyone know that while the physical word still holds sway, it's vital to journey into the virtual space if business goals are to be met. No doubt, the printed word is powerful, but the digital word wields the sword.

A popular misconception about the digital is that it drives away the physical. Especially where content is concerned, this, to most, means doing away with all printed publications and tra-ditional means of advertising. This misunderstanding is what delays the adoption of the digital, and very often, cramps its progress, if implemented.

This is completely untrue. Digital does not mean the absence of the physical-it only means taking the printed word to an alternate, parallel realm and allowing it to become more competitive and sought after. Print and digital always go together-they're both different sides of the same coin.

Taken together, they can be unstoppable-the catch is, businesses must know how to optimise the two and blend them where necessary. What usually happens is that companies do away completely with the physical aspect of content and adopt an extremely superficial, unfocused digital approach that gets them nowhere. Eventually, they shut shop completely, unable to cope with the vicissitudes of the changing market.

I've personally witnessed the rise and fall of a prominent print-first media organisation in one of the countries where I worked. This company refused pointedly to take its content operations online despite repeated advice to do so.

There came a point when all competing publications had a definite online niche, but this company stubbornly refused to follow, saying they did not have the budget to hire an entire digital team, or even upskill the existing ones.

For three years after the digital onslaught, they survived. Then, one fine day in October 2017, they announced to all unsuspecting staff who were busy finalising content for the next day that they were shutting down. The entire workforce was dismissed in one mighty blow and they let it be known that they had to stop as they could not continue working in all-print mode. All because they refused to acknowledge that the 'digital' had arrived!

2

WHY THIS FUSS ABOUT CONTENT?

*Digital means money; digital means endless;
digital means potential.*

So now we come to another pertinent question: why so much fuss around digital? Agreed, it's a new way of doing things, but why so much attention? Becasuse digital means money, digital means endless, digital means potential. As opposed to the traditional, 'barrier-rich' brick-and-mortar world, the digital realm with its seamlessness transcends time and space and connects people and ideas like never before. And when content enters this space with its power to transform thoughts and actions, is it any wonder that so much centers around it?

Traditionally, content was thought of as a communication tool, and its role as a marketing tool came much later, when the Internet and computers became household names. Businesses that had already discovered the power of the digital word began considering the possibility of using this to create brand awareness and increase sales. It is believed that the term "content marketing" originated in the mid-90's, and email marketing, websites and blogging were the primary tools used at the time.

With time, the idea of content marketing grew and expanded, and as social media platforms began to offer people instant visibility and the freedom to be creative, businesses began to further explore the hidden potential of content in the digital realm. And with the arrival of Facebook in 2003, the scene just exploded and the rest, they say, is history. Till date, Facebook continues to remain the platform of choice for marketing content, while Instagram, Twitter and LinkedIn follow close behind.

Then came video and YouTube. Suddenly, the public had access to videos at the click of a mouse and right there was born content marketing as we know it today. Social media and videos became instant tools to connect brands directly with audiences and forge better connections. Today, brands are making their presence felt across all social media platforms and constantly innovating on content creation and marketing techniques.

There's no doubt that content is king and the ability to create and market this content, the most in-demand skill around. The potential to experiment with content is immense, and virtual reality is all set to become more immersive, more engaging and more connected with the overall brand experience. Today, there is an increasing demand for digital content specialists with varying skills. From digital media photographers, writers, videographers, animators, strategists, game designers, analytics specialists, web developers, graphic designers-the potential to make your digital presence felt is endless.

The challenges of virtual content creation are many, and the first of these is the difference between content writing, content strategy and content marketing. All three concepts are inextricably related and one cannot exist without the other, yet, there are crucial differences and it is necessary to know what each term means, so that you can steer your business goals and sales targets accordingly. No entrepreneur can stand by and see his dreams crumble and die for want of proper planning. However, most businesses fail because they underestimate the power of their content—they fail to articulate their content goals and marketing tactics—as a result of which even the brightest of business ideas flounder and die.

THE STORY - 1

RADIANT CANDLES

I don't know where I went wrong, but there just was no sale.

Digital content is not only about getting random content out there in the virtual space-you need to put in lots of hard work and constantly be in the know of what your audience wants., if you wish to make a dent in the highly competitive, creative space.

Let's look at a venture that started not-too-long ago: A one-person enterprise that failed due to the lack of a clear content strategy, content goal, target audience and creativity.

Radiant Candles was small startup that began out of one room in a small city in India. The owner, Sachin, was a first-time entrepreneur, who quit a traumatic 9-5 job to be, in his words, "his own master and do something that satisfied his creative instincts."

Since he was good at sculpting things with clay and wax, he decided to make and sell candles in different shapes and sizes. Fragrant candles, heart-shaped candles, star shaped candles-his aim was to reach out to every special moment in people's lives. After all, whether it is a celebration, a funeral, or a special prayer, who wouldn't want a candle lighting up the occasion?

And so the candle making business began with much gusto and enthusiasm. With the support of his friends, Sachin got down to designing and making candles all by himself and for a while it gave him immense pleasure. Free from the shackles of a nine-to-five job, he spent days and nights immersed in the world of candles.

Soon, he had enough to start selling outside. Beautifully shaped candles, perfect for any occasion. But how could he convince people to buy his candles? In a city like his, every corner of every street had candle makers that could give his beauties a run for their money. So how could he stand out?

Sachin floundered. He knew he had to go digital to make his presence felt, but he had no idea how. Then, his friend, Rodney told him about a website designer friend, who, he said, would design a site for Radiant Candles at a reasonable cost. Two weeks and much brainstorming later, a regular, static website was born, with the images of candles, a contact number for orders, and a brief description about the business.

One month passed and there were no orders. Sachin put up his website details on his personal social media account, and spread the word. Still nothing. Enthusiasm soon turned to despair. The self-starter/entrepreneur idea didn't seem such a good idea after all. No one seemed to be able to help him, and Sachin just couldn't bear to think of getting back to his old job routine.

Desperate, he turned to his friend and former colleague, who advised him to think differently. Together, they came up with the idea of creating a video for Radiant Candles-a short, two-minute video that encapsulated Sachin's dream and visually told viewers how the candles were made, and how they could be used to brighten up any occasion.

Together, they aggressively targeted buyers on social media. One video became two. Two became three. They were sent out at random to all of their contacts, known and unknown, on social media. There were a few enquiries, but no solid sales.

Today, Sachin is back at work in a ten-five job, Radiant Candles just a memory. "It's just impossible to get people to buy stuff," he says. "I don't know where I went wrong, but there just was no sale, so I closed it down."

Sachin's story is familiar to most of us who today, are being catapulted from the physical to the virtual world at breakneck speed. Particularly post the pandemic, the digital realm has overwhelmed our lives, with everything that we knew before being turned topsy-turvy. Content is abundant and all around us, but with changes happening so fast, it has left us flummoxed and completely clueless about how to tap it.

Isn't it time we changed that?

THE STORY - 2

AMBER's CUPCAKES

Rather than give up, they decided to properly strategise and plan their social media content.

Amber is a housewife from Mangalore, a small town in India. A busy mom of two and the wife of a high-flying executive, she had no thoughts of starting out on her own as an entrepreneur until her children grew up and started school. A casual chat with her friend from next door, coupled with her love of baking, prompted her to begin her own cake business, specialising in cupcakes. She made and decorated them at home, and started out by catering to small private events by friends and family. Encouraged by the positive reviews, she decided to take her business to the next level.

Instead of taking the usual route and approaching the nearby bakeries and coffee shops for orders, Amber decided to target her customers directly. She began by join-

media groups for ladies and mothers, and participated actively in their conversations. She spoke about her cupcake business and about how cakes found in bakeries and shops are generally unhealthy. Her USP was the 'homemade & healthy' angle, where she stressed the need for families, especially children, to eat healthy while not having to forego sweet treats.

Gradually, Amber started receiving orders from these groups for birthday parties and weekend group outings. A couple of orders came in for wedding cakes. Her reputation as a reliable, affordable, health-focused baker grew.

Encourged and highly motivated by the response she was getting, Amber decided to go bigger.

She sought the help of her sister, Kaitlyn, a web designer. Together, they came up with a brand name: Amber's cupcakes. They created a colourful website with actual photographs of the cakes made. It had Amber's contact details and social media handles. There was even some lovely background music for those who preferred the complete sensory experience.

The sister duo went all out on social media, too. They made frequent, regular posts about Amber's cupcakes and invited everyone to try out the cakes to feel the difference. Complete with hashtags and visuals, they were all set to make a mark in the virtual space.

ing Facebook's local/community pages specific to her town. A month passed and business began to slow down. Apart from a few casual enquiries, there were no actual sales. It was then that Amber & Kaitlyn sat down and brainstormed. Rather than give up, they decided to properly strategise and plan their social media content. So they researched online, spoke to digital marketeers and came up with a solution: create a detailed plan of action-a content strategy.

This consisted of a content goal (promote Amber's Cupcakes by reaching out to as many people as possible), a target audience: (women between the ages of 25 & 50 and large corporates), type of content (static & videos), content distribution channels (Instagram, Facebook, Twitter), content posting frequency (daily), and a business mission: to attain 5000 social media followers in 3 months.

To achieve this goal, they created dedicated Facebook pages for baking and cake decoration. Amber also conducted regular baking workshops for adults and kids, and organised live sessions on social media where she answered queries from first-time bakers on cake making.

Her efforts did not end there. She and Kaitlyn created short, promotional videos to market Amber's Cupcakes. For this, they brought together family and friends who pitched in with testimonials about the cakes, and even enacted celebration scenes where the cupcakes were front and centre. These videos were posted independently, as well as with text, on social media. The videos kept coming, the posts were tailored to the specific social media platform.

When her audience grew and the demand for her baking classes went up, she made the sessions paid. When this was also well accepted, she went to the extent of announcing free online cupcake making classes for the first 10 people who signed up for it.

Needless to say, the strategy paid off, and today, Amber's cupcakes has a dedicated and fast-growing clientele who only order her "healthy, delicious" cakes for their special occasions.

What's the secret of Amber's success?

Strategy, vision, determination and the willingness to be flexible in her approach. She planned her content in detail, had a definite goal, and pursued it despite all odds.

Both stories have one takeaway: content planning. In today's digital marketplace, it's absolutely vital to strategise and plan your content before you do anything else. That makes all the difference and very often, is the ultimate decider in whether you continue with your entrepreneurial dreams or see them shatter before your very eyes.

Now do you see why content creation and marketing are no

child's play? Do you see that it is an area that demands extensive skill, expertise and planning?

Let's now re-examine the terms content writing, content strategy and content marketing. This book uses all three terms intercheangeably, so it's imperative to define the three terms and the connection between them.

3

WRITING vs STRATEGY vs MARKETING

*To get maximum impact out of your content,
use all three of them-one cannot exist without the other.*

It's easy to confuse the terms content writing, content strategy and content marketing. All the three concepts are inextricably related and one cannot exist without the other, yet, there are crucial differences and it is necessary to know what each term means, so that you can steer your business goals and sales targets accordingly.

Content writing is the act of "creating" content-it's the process of using words, visuals and audio to give concrete shape to your business. It's the most important way of letting your audience or potential customers know what you're offering, and how they can access them.

Content marketing, on the other hand, is the manner in which this content is used to create awareness of your brand, drive sales and get more customers. Content strategy is the way the "content creation" must be channelled and managed-it is a map of your content goals, a detailed identification of your target audience and the content they would prefer, as well as plans to deliver content to them in a way that attracts them to your brand. In other words, your content strategy should be the pillar around which you create and deliver your content, to let your audience know why you're unique and why they must prefer you over competition.

To get maximum impact out of your content, it is important to not just create content, but to also strategise and market it. The content that is created will have no effect if it isn't marketed well, or planned in detail. So before you attempt any kind of content whatsoever, decide how you will plan and market it. Many business ventures fail because they only create content without planning for it or marketing it afterwards.

If we analyse the case of Radiant Candles, the main cause of its downfall was the lack of a proper content strategy, creation and marketing plan. There was just a static website with the basic content and nothing else. Even the video idea, although contemporary, lacked vision and strategy, and a targeted delivery plan. As a result, it floundered and died. No entrepreneur can stand by and see his dreams crumble and die for want of proper planning. This is where the need for an integrated content strategy-creation-marketing plan comes in.

DIGI-PRENEUR

PROFILE - 1

Ruchika Nagpal Mehta
Founder, Patavya Diamonds

Ruchika has been using social media extensively to reach out to more people and help garner the traction that her business needs.

Instagram: Patavya Diamonds
Facebook: Patavya Diamonds

Ruchika Nagpal Mehta is an entrepreneur based in New Delhi, India. Founder and owner of Patavya Diamonds known for its original, breathtaking designs. Ruchika has been using social media extensively to reach out to more people and help garner the traction that her business needs.

"Since I was a newbie in the business, my friends and family were sceptical about I would pull this off without having a client base already, as other jewellers have business legacies spanning years and decades! However, I was confident that the marvels of technology would allow me to stand apart, excel and, in fact, overhaul the existing giants," she says.

Digital content and marketing have always been her number one marketing tool to reach thousands of people in one go just at a click of a button.

"All I need to do is select the content and press the 'upload' button and there u go — my business is digital," she adds.

According to her, the likes and comments that she gets for this ensures that people know the latest products and designs that her brand offers. It also helps boost her morale and encourages her to innovate.

In Ruchika's words:

"Facebook and Instagram have not only let me showcase my niche products to people I know, but the hashtags I use have helped me garner substantial views and reach out to random people who would just search for the word in my hashtag. In fact, the power of networking options - such as "viewed by friends," "by friends' friends" and "viewed by anyone" have created a different vertical for marketing and reaching out to millions in one go! Gone were the days for me when people used to take tens of years to create a client base, I was already confident that with the right use of social media, I'd be able to do the latter in few months which actually did, and translated into a hugely positive outcome for me."

4

INVESTING IN DIGITAL CONTENT

The right and relevant content marketing strategies can make or break your brand. It can build empires from nothing and even facilitate the collapse of major ones.

A digital identity is your business signature and the only passport to the growth of your entrepreneurial journey. Not too long ago, content writing was thought of as a 'copy-and-paste' activity. Any new entrepreneur, while brainstorming the other aspects of his business, would brush aside the digital content part of it saying: "that can be easily taken care of. Create a website, copy-paste something from the Internet, recruit a fresher to post something once in a while-that's no worry at all."

Content was always sacrificed at the altar of 'more important' aspects, and so it remained at best, an unnecessary process, something that didn't need too much attention.

However, times are changing and today, investing in digital content is the biggest favour any entrepreneur can do for his business. Content creation is no longer "just" an activity, it is the cornerstone of the growth and progress of any business venture. Not only does it require great skill and finesse, but it also requires a keen eye on the market, extensive research capabilities, a creative mindset and great agility. That's not all: Digital is twice as fast as print, both in implementation and impact. Also, to be able to keep pace with market trends and to know what your business needs, digital is more effective.

When it comes to digital content, plagiarism is a strict no-no. Perhaps, if businesses took content creation more seriously and focused on the content that they actually need, then plagiarism need never rear its ugly head. Then again, there are those who say that plagiarism comes about because there is no legitimate source for the digital content being churned out every day. Anyone can create a website or start a channel, and content is all around to be taken at will. But that's no excuse for second-hand, copied, rehashed content. Apart from the legalities involved, plagiarised content makes your business look cheap. Can you really build your brand and showcase its uniqueness with duplicate/plagiarised content? Your content has to convey your vision, strategy and goals. It drives your business growth and must be at the centre of your marketing and organisational strategy. Therefore, digital is no longer just an afterthought, it is an absolute necessity.

If you want great content, stop trivialising digital content creation. Invest in a great team that can translate your vision, plans and market goals into reality. This creates a positive perception, builds a favourable mindset for your brand in the market and equips consumers to make important decisions. The right and relevant content marketing strategies can make or break your brand. It can build empires from nothing and even facilitate the collapse of major ones. Entrepreneurs and businesses, particularly small ventures, cannot underestimate the power of a strong content strategy.

Hire people with vision and enthusiasm. Invest in the tools and platforms needed for its propagation. Make it the top priority in your business growth plans. Understand that the digital space is here to stay, remember that a digital identity is your business signature and the only passport to the growth of your entrepreneurial journey. Merely acknowledging the digital onslaught is not enough, businesses must be able to implement it into their daily operations.

5

WHY MARKET CONTENT?

Content marketing offers valuable information to targeted audiences who consume it when they want to.

To begin with, let's try and understand why content marketing in its new avatar, is the rage today. Why must we market content? Won't traditional ads do?

Fact is, the fast-growing, evolving digital content landscape requires a modern marketing approach. In contrast to the interruptive approach of traditional marketing where the company promoting the content interrupts a customer's daily routine to bombard information, content marketing, or the modern-day marketing approach, is subtler and more permissive, where customers or the consumers, are allowed to discover the content and use it whenever they want to. In short, content marketing is all about providing value to your customer rather than sell them a product or a service.

Traditional marketing channels consisted of newspaper & TV ads, billboards, email campaigns, brochures, fliers, banner ads and radio commercials. Content marketing uses a totally different but more powerful and permanent medium of distribution: social Media.

Traditional marketing did not bother with the kind of consumer they were feeding the content to-they sent out general information that targeted anyone and everyone. Content marketing, on the other hand, offers valuable information to targeted audiences, who consume it when they want to. In other words, the consumer is at the centre of the marketing strategy.

Content marketing engages in a conversation with the audience based on which content creators and marketeers know what the audience preferences are, what is relevant at that point of time and what the future trends are likely to be. It also allows content marketeers to refine their marketing strategies and focus on plans that work.

Not surprisingly, content marketing is also more affordable

than traditional marketing. According to a study by Demand Metric, content marketing costs 62% less than traditional marketing. It says that per dollar spent, content marketing generates approximately 3 times as many leads as traditional marketing. (DemandMatric)

That said, the number of people seeking out a product or service after reading content about it, is significant (60%, according to Demand Metric). Today, there is no business that does not know the power of content marketing: it's a fact that when you market your content, you ensure customer loyalty to your product or service, gain valuable market insights, get immediate reach and visibility and help understand market trends. In fact, it's more useful as a long-term strategy than the traditional model. And who doesn't wish to be ahead of the market, ahead of competition? (DemandMatric)

Content creators and marketeers say the transition from traditional marketing to content marketing is easier said than done but it's been proved that once you get into the thick of it and gain momentum, it's unstoppable and brings great rewards.

6

GETTING IT RIGHT

Good content must not be sourced or copied from elsewhere and must be a true reflection of what the individual or the organisation represents.

So, now you know why digital content is important and why it is imperative to have a content strategy-creation-marketing plan in place.

The next step is to know what content is right for you. Mistake it not, the content creation and marketing options are endless, so you need to know what works for you. Remember, content is anything that imparts information in any form-for example, even the picture of a smiling baby is content. But good content would be information that is relevant, timely and useful. In fact, it is content that is relevant for the person it is intended and disseminates information in an interesting manner. In short, good content is not just "interesting content," it is interesting content that is also useful.

So, how can we make sure content is relevant and good?

1.The first thing to consider here is something most people ignore: originality. Good content must be original. It must not be sourced or copied from elsewhere and must be a true reflection of what the individual or the organisation represents. This needs time and attention, so make sure you plan your content activities with enough time for original thought.

That's not all. Your writing style also needs to be original. For this, you could use personal experiences or anecdotes to pepper your narrative. Even if you're writing marketing material, a touch of the personal will add more depth.

2. Create content that is specific for your target audience: Content often gets 'lost' in a quagmire of generalities. There's so much information being bandied around, that neither the author nor the reader knows what to take in and what to leave out. This is one of the biggest mistakes content creators make. Decide what exactly you wish to say, and say it.

3. Decide what the goal of your content is-does it force the audience to read more about what you have said? Does it force them to sign up for your services? Does it interest them enough to want to share it with their friends? Evaluate your content to see if it answers these questions.

4. Make sure your content is focused and answers a question. Look at it this way: If you need information, won't you look it up on Google?

Similarly, create your content in such a way that if someone needs information about that particular product or service, they will refer to your content. If you manage to do this, then you can be rest assured your content is good.

5. Make sure your content is well-researched and sourced-Any content, short or long, pictorial or written, MUST be the result of extensive thought and study. Well-researched content always speaks for itself and the audience is immediately able to relate to it. One way to do this would be to read up as much as possible about your content. Then, make sure you use trusted, reliable sources. Third, if you're using someone else's information, make sure you acknowledge it.

 6. Ensure that your content is "different"-it should not only be original, but should also have a unique point of view. What's the point using a focal point that others have already highlighted?

This is where your imagination comes in, being able to spin the same content in a different manner, so as to make it seem refreshing and unique. Hint: Think of a different angle to explain the same thing. Appeal to people's emotions, make them think, make them question existing paradigms. Never make your content text-only. Remember: visuals, especially videos, add much to the overall impact.

DIGI-PRENEUR

PROFILE - 2

Gunjandeep Singh
Founder, Aroma Souls

Aroma Souls deals in essential oils, aromatic oils and handmade candles made out of soy wax and blended with various essential oils.

www.aromasouls.com
https://instagram.com/aroma.souls?utm_medium=copy_link
https://www.facebook.com/aromasoulsforyou/
https://twitter.com/AromaSouls

Gunjandeep Singh founded Aroma Souls in 2018. He is a certified aromatherapist and a wellness coach.

Aroma Souls deals in handmade candles made with soy wax and blended with various essential oils which are customisable.

He has used social media and digital platforms extensively to market and promote the Aroma Souls brand name and build awarness about the product and its benefits and build up a strong brand in a short span of three years or so.

Essential oils are liquids extracted from a plant source that is later converted into oil through the process of distillation. These oils come with a natural fragrances that have therapeutic properties. Due to their rising popularity, these oils are made available through multiple channels.

7

THE DOS & DON'TS

Poor content lacks a clear buyer persona and does not highlight how your product or service will be useful to the customer.

Identifying 'bad' or 'poor' content is another way to understand 'what works.

Poor content is anything that is unplanned, done in haste and lacks vision and clarity. Poor content does not take into account SEO principles (we'll analyse that later), it does not motivate the audience or consumer to follow-up or act, it lacks variety, does not tell a story or resonate with them, and it lacks variety in delivery and style.But, most importantly, poor content indulges in shameless self-promotion. It focuses on the product and not on the user experience. Remember, your customer is the star of your content writing & marketing exercise-every word, every detail, should appeal to their senses, and not flaunt your product in their face.

Poor content also lacks clarity about the audience they're targeting. It lacks a clear buyer persona and does not highlight how your product or service will be useful to the customer. It lacks visual impact, comparisons and contrasts and ends abruptly, leaving the audience with a feeling of incompleteness and an "Okay, so what?" effect.Let's look at an example of badly written content and the same content written well, taking the example of Radiant Candles.

POOR CONTENT

Radiant Candles-bringing you a wide range of candles in different shapes and sizes at affordable prices, for different occasions. Our prices range from Rs 500-Rs 1000 and can be attractively gift wrapped according to your preference. We're the first in the market offering custom-made candles for different occasions.

GOOD CONTENT

Who can underestimate the power of a candle? The quiet unassuming source of light for every occasion-be it a fun party, a birthday get-together, a family reunion, a funeral or even a romantic dinner-the candle is a man's best friend.

If you'd like to know more about how you can use the humble candle to add light to your life, get in touch with us at Radiant Candles. We'll make sure your memories last a lifetime. What's more, our design experts will guide you about the right candle design for the right occasion and make sure your every preference is accounted for.

Count on us for the light-and watch the shadows disappear!

8

CONQUERING THE CONTENT FEAR

*Once you've decided to establish a digital identity and signature
and decided on the type of content you prefer,
embark on a diversification strategy.*

All said and done, content creation and marketing can be daunting for many. It's easy to give tips and provide guidelines, but how does one know that one is on the right track and doing the right thing, to achieve the right effect?

Most organisations take on content writers and marketeers and assign them impossible KPIs without knowing whether these strategies are actually making a difference. As a result, the employees struggle and the business struggles, with no positive outcomes whatsoever.

In my opinion, once you've decided to establish a digital identity and signature and decided on the type of content you'd prefer, go on a diversification mode. Content diversity is as important as originality, if the desired outcomes are to be met. Don't be afraid to experiment, to try out different content types.

Let's say, for instance, that you've done some solid research about the content you're about to produce. Your aim is to write a beautiful, engaging blog. But instead of an all-text blog, why not create a stunning infographic with the information you've collected? Or produce the same content as text, infographic, memes, newsletters, pictures and maybe even as a quiz? In all probability, you'll be able to generate twice as many business leads, which will help make informed decisions.

It is important to remember the 80-20 rule when formulating a content framework. This means that your content, whatever its form (video, audio, text), should only be 20% promotional, the rest should be informative, engaging and educational. The last thing your audience wants is to 'waste' time watching/listening to/reading about a product-instead, pique their interest and make them look up the product or service you're offering, by telling them 'why' they should buy it (this should take up 80% of your content creation ratio).

So, instead of telling your audience that you have a new product/service that they can opt for, pitch it to them by telling them how their business will benefit with the new product and why it's a game changer.

Don't be afraid to ask for feedback from your customers. This is the best way to understand where your content is going-no amount of analytics, no in-depth analysis, can actually measure up to an assessment from your audience about your content. Put up regular surveys-this can be done for videos too. Ask them direct questions upfront: "what do you like about my content?" "what isn't working?" "what would you like to see more of?"

These are not fool-proof tips, but they're sure-fire ways to get you started on the right track. Ultimately, success or failure depends on you-your commitment, patience and willingness to adapt, innovate and change.

DIGI-PRENEUR

PROFILE - 3

Debabrata Mandal
Founder, DM India

*DM India is an AGRO-FARM product
marketing start up*
www.dmindia.org
App: DM India (Google Play Store)
India Mart
https://www.indiamart.com/debabratamsd-india-opc-private-limited/

Debabrata Mandal launched DM India in 2019. It was set up with the objective of improving the availability of clean, healthy graded fruits and vegetables to consumers at best prices through doorstep delivery.

Over a period of three years since its establishment, DM India, based out of Murshidabad in India's West Bengal, registered significant growth.

The company is dedicated to serving small agro-farm producers for better access to markets through its network of partners across India and the neighbouring South Asian countries.

"Ever since inception, DM India has been growing as a pan Indian entity. It exports agro-farm products to the neighbouring countries of South Asia and is now in talks with traders from the Middle East to meet their organic farm produce directly procured from farmers," says Mandal.

DM India has an extensive network of small farmers across the Eastern Indian states, particularly in the hilly regions. With the help of these small farmer producers and their cooperatives, DM India procures all kinds of vegetables, pulses, spices, fruits, dry fruits, food-grains and millets.

They also supply certified organic produce, which is their mainstay.

In order to get the reach he needed, Mandal explored various business models. As the first step, he ensured his online presence on digital platforms and local digital business directories including *GoogleMyBusiness*. He also created his own website and App, DM India, which is available for download on Google Playstore. DM India is actively present on India-Mart, Facebook-Marketplace and several other platforms, which generates leads from across India, South Asia and the Middle East.

According to Mandal, the investments that he made towards digital asset creation continues to make a difference in his entrepreneurial journey. In his opinion, digital presence is crucial in enhancing profits and ensuring a steady income for his partners, who comprise mainly small farmers.

9

PRINT vs DIGITAL

The main target is your audience and that's who you're seeking to impress.

Now that we've seen how important content is and how critical it is for that content to be "good," let's look at the different types of content and why they should be treated differently. This is important, because most people treat the different content platforms as one and the same-that is, they think that one single type of content can be created for all content platforms-print, web, social media and visual/video.

WHY is it important to think differently for different platforms? The main target is your audience, and that's who you're seeking to impress. With that goal, if you look around, you'll see a distinct divide in audience preferences. There will be people who prefer the traditional long-form text, while there will be another chunk of the population that prefers the short-text, visual-must form-this is what you'd find across most social media platforms. The much-travelled business executive would prefer infographics, while the younger generation may prefer only visuals. It is, therefore, important to treat each content platform as unique with its own identity.

The other often overlooked reason is the evolution of print vs digital content.. If you take time to think about how one evolved from the other, you'll realise the need to see all content platforms differently.

Print used to be the ONLY medium of information and communication till around ten years ago. You had your newspapers and magazines with printed texts and an image or two to accompany the piece. You subscribed to these periodicals (so called because they were published at a certain periodic interval) and they arrived regularly at your doorstep. You also found them at airports and train stations, and you bought them to fill in time during the journey. The text was in long-form and had an introduction about the information that was to follow, then it had an analysis portion, followed by a conclusion of whatever was said until then. The upside: you could read them at leisure and keep them stocked at home for ready reference if ever you felt the need. The flip side: any updates to the information could come in only as quickly as the newspapers or the media could publish them.

Then came digital: instant, fast and informative. Immediate access was available for updates, sources and different perspectives for the same issue, complete with visuals both still and moving. The world became smaller and information, easier to obtain. Long-form was out and the visual aspect took over, big time.

Writing for both mediums, therefore, took on different paradigms. Writing for print became time consuming and less preferred, while the fast and furious pace of the digital world suited many. 'Writers' became 'content creators' as content also diversified. With each content form came different content requirements. And content creation took on a whole different meaning altogether.

That said, let's take a look at the different digital content platforms and how to approach them.

10

SOCIAL MEDIA PLATFORMS & CONTENT

Each social media platform is unique-it allows users to post certain kinds of content while disallowing others.

Everyone has a general idea about what social media is, but very few know what to do with it. To most people, social media is a vast digital space to exchange news and views and connect with friends. What they don't know is that not all social media platforms are the same: content on each platform is created differently and the expectation from each of these platforms is different. We'll discuss more about social media in chapter 15, but before that, it's important to understand how different all its platforms are. Imagine you're scrolling through Twitter feeds. You wouldn't expect to see a lengthy video that will keep you entertained: what you'd expect to see are short, terse texts of around 260 characters or so, with a text or a short few-second video to accompany it. Similarly, when you browse Instagram, you'd expect a photograph or a video to do the talking, with some text as an add-on, or sometimes no text at all. With Facebook, you expect a mixed bag, but again, more visual than text heavy. LinkedIn, on the other hand, is more popular as a job hunting/networking platform, so you'd expect posts and videos on career trajectories and tips to land the right job, than, say, a birthday celebration video. Then again, each social media platform allows users to post different kinds of content while disallowing others. So it's a mixed bag-one you must understand properly in order to create the right kind of content. Let's look at each of these in turn:

Facebook: Facebook is all about emotions-capturing the ins and outs of your life and those of your friends, in all its colour and variety. It is about creating a "connection," a "rapport," that allows you to send and receive friend requests and if mutually accepted, become part of a network that you regularly browse, to see what everyone is up to. And so, by its inherent "informal" nature, it is easy to see that short videos and blogs would hit home effectively. The language is casual and friendly, and slangs and dialects all find a place.

Here, it's essential to capture the interest or attention of the audience in the first few words, or the early seconds of the video.

Remember, a Facebook user is only casually browsing and so will only pause for texts or videos that capture his/her attention. Example: "Let's make a delicious 5-minute dinner that will wow the family." Or "Here's why you should not ignore a persistent headache."

Instagram: While Facebook is more about creating a "connection," Instagram is more for "observation." Although informal in nature, an Instagram user is not exactly looking for updates about a friend, he/she is trying to figure out what the latest trends are and looking for lifestyle tips or inspirational quotes. For instance, a particular make-up look, or a weekend getaway. Or a life quote from a real-life hero. So, content should focus more on the "how" than the "what." Example: "How to achieve that sultry-eyed look for evening parties." OR "What to do in Georgia with just $50."

Twitter: This is a platform to let the world know what you think of whatever is happening around you. You can be objective, analytical, sarcastic or humorous, depending on your views. This is more of a formal than an informal platform, so the language is more formal and elevated. Bear in mind that there is a word count, so if you're thinking of writing an essay, this is probably not the place. Example: The Covid-19 booster vaccine shot is much needed, but is Omicron the only variant to be worried about? Will the booster keep away other strains? The accompanying visual could be abstract, like a STOP! sign, or more specific, like a syringe with a question mark over it.

LinkedIn: Probably the most formal of all the platforms. The purpose here is to build "networks" for business promotion or for landing a job. The language is highly elevated and business-like. The visual can be straightforward, like a person speaking, or a highly suggestive one where the audience is led gradually to the answer. Example: Is your CV outdated? How can you tell? The visual could either be a photograph of a traditional printed CV with a line struck across it, or a video where a prospective candidate creates a video CV and sends it to an employer. Suppose, let's say, you're advertising your photography business. Think about which text-video combination would be more effective for which platform, and why:

A video shows you facing away from the screen, against a popular tourist monument with a camera slung around your neck, clicking one picture after another. Suddenly, you turn and say: "Hi, I'm a photographer based in London. I take all kinds of pictures in a professional, colourful manner. I'm affordable, too, check me out." Your email and contact details appear on screen.

OR

A video that shows a series of occasions in rapid succession-a flowery field, a baby's smiling face, a bride and a funeral. The sound of the clicking camera for each occasion. A two-second pause. All images in a collage on the screen. A voice that utters a single sentence: "Capture life in all its glory. Contact (name and number)." A voice that utters a single sentence: "Capture life in all its glory. Contact (name and number)."

11

THE IMPORTANCE OF STRATEGY

Content creation is a well-thought out, well-planned endeavour that requires creativity, out-of-the box thinking and a clear eye on the future.

Why strategy? Now that know what makes for good content, isn't that enough? MUST content be strategised?

Yes, it must. Any content today, MUST have a strategy.

We know by now that content is king. But how many of us realise that the king is totally defenseless without his soldiers? Just him in his sartorial splendour is nothing but a sitting duck for enemy attack: what makes him strong is his military power, a stable throne and a kingdom that has his back. The same goes for content: It can be perfectly crafted/produced and well promoted, but unless it has a strategic vision and features that give it a magic touch, it's a dud.

So, what makes for great digital content? An ABSOLUTELY VITAL aspect of great content is a comprehensive content creation strategy. Content is NOT meant to be created at random, rather, it's a well thought out, well-planned endeavor that requires creativity, out-of-the box thinking, and a clear eye on the future.

So, what's the first step to creating a great content strategy? Let me try and explain this with an example from my professional experience.

Many years ago, when digital content creation was in its infancy, I worked for a media organisation where I was part of a brand promotion campaign. We were given specific goals, and my role was to make sure that the content that came out fit the brief. My team worked tirelessly. We brainstormed, worked nights, weekends and every free hour. We hired the best copywriters and content creators-by all accounts we were on the road to brand stardom. But when the campaign went live, it didn't create the impact it was expected to. The bosses were disappointed and our team which was expecting glory and fireworks, was dejected and demotivated. But then, a heated post-mortem debate showed us that the campaign was focused ONLY on the brand and NOT on the consumer. While it bombarded its target audience with the company's mission, vision and cutting-edge, futuristic products, it forgot the ONE MAIN thing that would have turned the whole experience around: THE CUSTOMER. While we were busy creating a brand identity and feeding the audience with what we wanted, we forgot to figure out whether it was what the customer actually needed. So, in the end, despite a flamboyant, high-visibility campaign, we failed to take off. Now, on hindsight, it is obvious that instead of asking ourselves what would be convenient for us to produce, we should have asked what brings value to the audience.

That was years ago. Unfortunately, even today, many media companies STILL fail to hero their customers/readers. So keen they are on SELF-PROMOTION that they forget the first cardinal rule of a good content strategy: The audience.

DIGI-PRENEUR

PROFILE - 4

Vighnesh Jha
Director, HUM SHILPAKAR

*HUM SHILPAKAR works for reviving waning arts
and crafts of India by providing the artisans a DIGITAL
IDENTITY, through which a means for business continuity,
stable income, greater sales and seamless connectivity with new
customers and markets.*

*Email: activistvighnesh@gmail.com
Twitter @vj4development
Facebook: Hum Shilpakar/We the Artisans*

Hum Shilpakar is a project initiated by Vighnesh Jha, a social entrepreneur from Bihar, India. *The project aims at facilitating digital transformation and providing an online platform for artisans, craftsmen and micro-entrepreneurs. It focuses on reviving nine hundred waning arts and crafts of India by providing the artisans and communities behind these art forms a digital identity and a means for business continuity, stable income, greater sales and seamless connectivity with new customers and markets.* For Vighnesh Jha, who is a Gandhian in spirit, "Hum Shilpkaar" is a dream project. He says it directly addresses the issues that were close to Mahatma Gandhi's heart and is a pathway to attain rural self-sufficiency or "Gram-Swaraaj."

For micro-enterprises at the bottom of the pyramid, enabling artisans for operating e-commerce platforms is critical for sustainability and business continuity, according to Vighnesh. At the moment, *"Hum Shilpakaar" is working to link the works of artisans with the market using digital platforms, such as Flipkart, Amazon and many more.* They're in the process of launching their "Facebook-mart" to promote Indian skills and art & craft, which will then be followed by a business app and its own dedicated digital platforms.

12

KNOWING YOUR AUDIENCE

Marketing professionals must coordinate and distribute different types of content through the right sales channel that will make sure customers get what they want.

We've seen how the audience/customer is at the centre of modern-day content creation. Therefore, knowing your audience profile is the first step towards a sucessful content creation strategy. There are many ways to understand your audience. First of all, the content strategist, along with the marketing head, MUST answer the following questions when deciding what kind of content should be created:

1)   What kind of content is the customer looking for? (NOT what kind of content are competitors churning out?)
2)   Why does he want this content?
3)   How exactly does he wish to interact with this content?

Here, it must be said that customer awareness and interest levels vary, so the content created must encourage the customer to respond to it and also spark a certain curiosity in him that makes him want to come back for more. To do this, always, look at the customer's journey from the point of view of the customer-this will help bring focus and clarity to the content creation process. In fact, studies show that customer experience overtakes both product and price as the deciding factor for brand success or failure.

I've worked in a company where it was the duty of the content creators to randomly create and publish a minimum of two content pieces everyday-all they had to do was find out what was trending and go with the flow. So, there was this group of content writers who racked their brains every morning to come up with ideas on what to write-they were more keen on meeting their KPIs rather than figuring out what actually worked. Needless to say, the company struggled and came up with several tactics to get the attention of the market, but they failed. Recently, they shut down.

I've also worked in a company where the entire team (marketing and content) sat together every morning, content plan in hand, reiterating their commitment to their customers and brainstorming the kind of content to create. Their content plan was comprehensive, flexible and futuristic, with a customer experience map outlining the different customer touch points and the kind of interactions with those touch points. Each writer was challenged to go beyond his/her comfort zone to reach out to the customer in different ways. The KPIs were not the focus-what counted was the collective effort at enhancing their customer experience. Their efforts paid off: In a short while, the website had a large reader base that actively commented on, interacted with and even gave feedback about the kind of content they'd want to see in future. As a result, the company's brand promotion campaigns also clicked. Today, the company has its presence in US, Europe, India and Saudi-Arabia and they're growing fast.

In this context, it wouldn't be amiss to say that the marketing department of a company also plays a huge role: They bridge the gap between sales and the customer. While in the past this meant getting results with traditional marketing tools and ad spends, today it means ensuring that the customer's online experience is seamless, relevant and resonating. In other words, marketing professionals must coordinate and distribute different types of content through the right sales channel that will make sure customers get what they want.

13

CUSTOMER EXPERIENCE MAP

Stop thinking of content strategy as just an excel sheet filled with data or text.

No content creation company that means business can afford to ignore a customer experience map. Yet, studies show that most companies are unaware of this need. A customer experience map must be the most powerful weapon in the hands of content creators and they must use it as often as possible to add value to their content. Here's a fact, unfortunate but true: Every customer would most probably have experienced pain of some kind with the companies they do business with. This pain could be a minor one, but it would certainly affect the quality of the experience. However, businesses often overlook the minor pain points and choose to focus only on the deal breakers or major issues, which could, in the long run, lead to the erosion of the existing customer base.

This is where the customer experience map comes in handy: it gives organisations a clear picture of the various ways in which customers interact with their business and helps analyse whether enough is being done to address them. In short, a customer experience map helps companies plan their customer experience and content consumption journeys, in ways that increase customer loyalty and satisfaction.

Now, you might ask how the customer experience map has anything to do with content creation and strategy. This is where the content creation strategisation process needs to be looked at as a detailed and intricate process, way beyond the confines of a simple excel sheet filled with content goals and aims. A customer experience map should be interwoven into the content strategy, so that the organisation gets a holistic view of the customer's experience across its various business channels and touchpoints.

When planning a content strategy, make sure to include the customer experience map as one of the goals/acheievables. Ask yourself how the content that you create and market can help ease the customer journey for your organisation. Begin by breaking down the exact points where a customer begins and interacts with the organisation. Move on to the different ways this journey branches out into—the various content 'interaction' points such as newsletters, emails, social media and so on. The map should then analyse the exact points where these content interaction journeys occur: do they occur at the initial stage of content awareness about the company, or do they occur at the stage where they make purchasing decisions, or at the loyalty stage where they decide to come back to your company for the same product?

At every stage, consider how the customer receives the information you provide: What do they think of it? Does the content that you provide ease their journey within your company, from one stage to the other? Does it address their pain points and give them enough clarity to make informed decisions? If not, how can the content be modified so as to make a better impact?

Once you begin to consider the csutomer experience map as an integral part of your content creation journey, you'll be amazed at the value addition that it brings. You'll find that the content is in complete alignment with the customers' needs and that your business has taken on the wings that it needs. Try it out.

14

SEO-THE KEY TO GETTING FOUND

Finding keywords for your content isn't too difficult if you know what's happening around you.

Modern-day content writers, strategists and marketeers cannot ignore the one word that drives everything around: Search Engine Optimisation or SEO. Ironically, however, SEO is very often underrated, ignored or an afterthought, because of which content never gets optimised.

Research shows that an overwhelming 95% of people look only at the first page of results that a search engine (Google) throws up, and of those, half the clicks go to the first three results. Wouldn't you want your content to be up there?

Basically, SEO is all about enhancing the quality and quantity of your website traffic, making sure that your content ranks high on Google and shows up on top of search options as soon as someone searches for content similar to yours. For instance, if your content is about home-made food delivery services, SEO best practices will ensure that your content will show up right on top when a potential customer searches Google for "food delivery services."

One mistake that most of us make is that we create websites without making it relevant for the audience that visit it. This is a futile exercise, because even a visually stunning website will completely collapse if there is nothing productive that comes out of it.

SEO is an excellent way to ensure that your content and therefore, your brand, stays relevant and visible. With the right use of SEO, you are able to understand what people are looking for online, the exact words they use and the content they prefer. This, in turn, will help you connect better with your customers and offer them the product or the service they need.

In order to get the maximum benefit out of SEOs, pay attention to keywords. Use keywords your audience is searching for. In fact, pepper your content with keywords. Use them in the title. Use them in the blurbs or the meta descriptions. Use keywords within the first 100 words of your content. Keep using the keyword(s) throughout the article, but let it flow naturally. The flip side of this is that if you get your keyword wrong, you'll hurt your business. You will miss out on free, unpaid web traffic (also known as "organic" traffic), and this will consequently mean fewer leads and fewer sales.

A good way to start using keywords would be to do keyword research. This is the only way you can identify the words or type of content that people are looking for. Keyword research is also a good focal point around which your content strategy can be structured.

The ideal practice would be to focus each piece of your content on a different keyword and to avoid using the same keyword twice. This will ensure that your contents don't compete with each other to show up high in search rankings.

Finding keywords for your content isn't too difficult if you know what's happening around you. Brainstorm with teammates, or even alone, about what the topics are, that would interest your potential audience.

Even if you have a very specific product or service that you're offering, there will be topics of interest within your business, it's your job to figure out what they are. Keep a list of words or phrases that keep coming up from time to time. Think of market trends, think of what everyone's talking about, and you have your keywords right there. You can then google these terms to zero-in on related terms or the exact words that searchers are looking for.

If you're a regular blogger, for instance, you'll be writing on a specific area or broad subject, and so your keyword brainstorming will revolve around these topics. If you're a first-time entrepreneur, your research will revolve around market trends or sales talk.

Another way to think of keywords would be to put yourself in your customers' shoes. Think of what they'd prefer. Come up with words/ideas. Do a Google search to come up with related terms that people are searching for, and voila! you have your keyword.

15

VIDEO CONTENT-THE BEST WAY TO TELL YOUR STORY

Very often, content creators devote time and attention to a video, however, they forget to engage with the viewers.

There's no medium more powerful than the video when it comes to marketing the service or product of a business or organisation. Video communication is direct and resonates with the customer like nothing else does. Video content is a surefire way to reach out to your target audience and get good Returns On Investment (ROI) because it captures emotions and instantly tells the customer why he must invest in a particular product or service. Needless to say, it's the best way to use content to get more leads and eventually, to build and consolidate a brand. There are many kinds of videos that can be used to create and market content and several platforms which allow such content to be streamed and distributed.

We're familiar with some of them, but before we proceed further, it is imperative to touch upon the most loved and used platform to create and market videos-YouTube, the second largest search engine after Google. It is the largest platform on which people upload videos, and it is the best opportunity today, to reach a large and diverse global audience. Although it was originally thought of as an entertainment channel, today, YouTube has become a critical tool for businesses and content marketeers to ensure maximum reach and visibility for their brand(s). The YouTube subscriber base has risen steadily over the years and a rising number of people prefer videos to text. In fact, studies say that over than a quarter of Internet users spend time on YouTube, and that it reaches over 2 billion users in over 75 languages.

Look at it this way: YouTube brings together two of the most potent online marketing tools-SEO and visuals. That's why it's important to know how to optimise content creation on You-Tube for maximum impact. In fact, YouTube content creation guidelines can serve as a standard guideline for creating and marketing any kind of video on any platform. The first thing to remember before you embark on a video creation journey is to be patient and set aside time to plan, create and edit your content. We know by now how important it is to plan. Video planning is even more important: it requires a realistic estimate of timelines to brainstorm, ideate, implement and edit the content footage. All of these cannot be done in one day, so you need to have realistic estimates in place.

While making a video of whatever kind, ask yourself the question: Why MUST people watch it? How is my content promotion better than that of my competition? Even if your subject is different, see how you can treat it differently. Look for interesting angles. Appeal to the emotions, evoke memories, strike a chord.

Keep it Short and Simple: When you make your video, make sure the message is simple, direct and easy to fathom. There is a lot of research that suggests that short videos (around 2-3 minutes) receive more views than the longer ones (over 5 mts). However, you're the best judge of your content, so figure out what works best in terms of video length.

Have a Title that Attracts Instant Attention: A title is the most important part of any content-it's the only way to let the audience know what the content is all about. So make sure the title of your video is informative and precise-keep it short and meaningful. Pay attention to keywords, just as you would do for written content.

Vivid Content Description: A title should be followed by a brief description of what your video is about-make this as descriptive and attractive as possible. Focus on how the video or the product/service you're offering will be useful to the audience. Don't forget to add links to your website.

Create Attractive Thumbnails: Thumbnails are an instant way to woo the audience and let them know in an instant, what the video is all about. So, make sure you create eye-catching, high-quality thumbnails that engage the viewers instantly.

Optimise your Video for Mobile Viewing: Users prefer viewing content on their mobiles rather than on their laptops, and so it is best if you get your video content suitable for mobile screen viewing.

Make Sure to create a Video Sitemap: A video gives Google information about the videos that are there on your website, so that Google can catalogue them correctly. Sitemaps help Google identify the most important parts of the video-basically, which page should be considered the "home" of the video. When someone Googles that video, the "homepage" is what Google search would link to.

Social Proof your video: Make sure to use Social Proof for your videos-Social Proof is basically a testimonial from users about how they find your video helpful. You can create social proofs in many different ways: Within the main video, you can show the number of views, or the number of votes, or likes of your video. For this, you can either have a static version or a dynamic version that shows a moving band with numbers going up.

Another idea would be to feature videos where users or customers recommend your products or services. There is no greater endorsement than positive user reviews, so this is one surefire to make sure your brand stands out.

Call to Action: It's not just enough to have a catchy video for your business; it is imperative that the video translates into leads and action on the part of the customer. For this, your video must contain a clear call to action. Invite the viewer to buy your product or your service-for this, you can either make the video's speakers invite them directly, or add a link prompting viewers to click on it, or even create a share button.

Decide on a Time to Publish the Video: Depending on what your product or service is, decide when it would be best to publish the video so that it can garner the maximum views. The more views you get, the more video platforms will recognise its significance and the more traction it receives. Offer an incentive to encourage viewers to buy your product or service-offer a special discount for the first 50 buyers. Or links to a free course. Freebies are ALWAYS attractive and will ensure more visitors to your website which in turn, may result in more sales.

Once you're done with the creation of the video, make sure you upload it to as many platforms as possible, not just your website. Don't also forget to share it to Facebook, Instagram, Pinterest, Twitter and LinkedIn. Then again, you could embed your video link to all the official emails you send out. If needed, pay Facebook and YouTube to reach a larger, more targeted audience.

While YouTube remains the most obvious video platform of choice, there are also other popular platforms like Vimeo, Twitch, TikTok or IGTV by Instagram, worth looking at. In fact, TikTok is fast emerging as the most preferred content creation and consumption platform today.

Very often, content creators devote time and attention to the video, however, they forget to engage with the viewers. This is where you could make a difference-remember to respond to their feedback and comments under your video-customers feel valued when their opinions are heard and responded to.

YouTube Driving the 'Creator Economy'

" YouTube has led to the birth of one of the largest digital trends in the modern world-the 'creator economy,' which refers to an eclectic range of content creators, community builders, bloggers, video makers, curators and social media influencers from across the world who use this platform to share their experiences and communicate their message with the world. The trigger for this was the YouTube Partner Program (YPP) which began in 2007 by sharing the revenue directly with its creators. Today, the number of creators on YPP is believed to have crossed 2 million worldwide, and the opportunities here are endless. The power of this ecosystem to help creators make money doing what they love, is attracting thousands to it every day.

YouTube is constantly innovating on its offerings, and today provides over ten different ways to make money. In just the last three years alone, it has paid over \$30 billion to artists, creators and media firms.

Despite lockdowns that interrupted so many creative industries throughout 2020, Oxford Economics research found that YouTube's creative ecosystem supported 394,000 full-time equivalent jobs in the US, an increase of 14 percent over 2019. In fact, the total contribution of YouTube's creative ecosystem to the US GDP was $20.5 billion in 2020, a 23 percent increase over 2019."

Source: Oxford Economics Research Report on Creator Economy

16

SOCIAL MEDIA CONTENT

Consistency is THE KEY to effective social media content and you must ensure that you post at regular intervals so that you engage with your audience.

Social Media is a vast ocean and creating and marketing content here is arguably the most challenging yet most rewarding experience for businesses. It is the battleground that determines success or failure, and hence requires considerable skill, patience, determination and in-depth knowledge to navigate.

Perhaps the most important thing to remember here is that content creation is a dynamic process. It changes with changing preferences and your strategy and marketing goals will automatically change as a result.

That said, the first rule of social media content is to identify your goal. What do I hope to achieve with my content, on social media? How will I leverage this content to achieve my sales targets?

Whatever the goals, make sure they're realistic, attainable, specific, relevant, measurable and deadline-bound. The more specific and detailed your goals are, the more effective they will be.

Some examples of smart goals are: 'My company will aim to increase the number of target group followers on Twitter by 200 next month.' OR 'We will aim to increase our video views by 10% by the end of this quarter.' These goals are achievable in the time frame mentioned, measurable and relevant for business success.

What is NOT realistic would be: 'My company will aim to reach 500K followers across all social media platforms by the end of this month.' OR 'We will work to translate every single website click into sales by the end of the quarter.'

Once you identify your goals, the next step is to create a plan to implement these goals. This is where an effective social media strategy comes into play. This helps you visualise the aforementioned goals, the marketing tactics you will use to attain them, and the manner in which you will track the progress and implementation of your strategies.

This is where most businesses struggle: very often, the lack of an effective social media strategy means that they create great content but fail to market it effectively. Or, they pay more attention to marketing tactics than the actual content, as a result of which the final impact becomes weak and ineffective. One of the most important questions that businesses struggle must answer today is: "How do I create a social media marketing strategy that is both realistic and ambitious? How do I make it work?" There is no fool-proof reply here, yet, there are some things that have been tried and proven to work.

Social Media Calendar: This is a useful tool to plan your content, as well as its publishing frequency and mode of delivery. The calendar can be in the form of a Google calendar or a spreadsheet or even an interactive dashboard.

While the specific details of a social media calendar may vary, it must contain aspects like the actual posts and the dates and time of these posts, the platform(s) on which these posts are intended to go live, what creative element (photo or video) will accompany each post and the links and hashtags to be used in each post. Certain social media platforms even allow you to schedule posts in advance, and this can be planned in the calendar, too. In short, a content creator, strategist and marketer must be able to get a clear roadmap about the entire social media schedule of a particular content, in one go. Maintaining a social media calendar helps you plan your content thoroughly, avoid repetitions and extra fluff, typos and grammatical errors and also the need for constant inspiration and ideas to make your posts work. Carefully planned content has its own appeal and the effect when compared with shoddy, hastily planned content is stark.

The one important aspect of a social media calendar is to make sure your posts are consistent. Consistency is THE KEY to effective social media content and you must ensure that you post at regular intervals so that you engage with your audience. While on social media, remember to tell a story and never to sell. Even if you are actually advertising your product or service, never make it obvious that you're selling it. Make your audience think they're watching a short movie. Or reading a story. Connect with them. Provide information and pique their interest. Make it look like you're here to solve their problems. Appeal to their emotions. Create a feeling of trust. Today's social media users crave a sense of community; they need to feel that they belong. So make sure you create content that is creative, appealing and informative.

TikTok Creator Fund

"TikTok Creator Fund rewards creators for doing what they do best — making incredible TikTok videos. It's TikTok's way of celebrating and supporting creators for their dedication, ingenuity, and spirit. Through the TikTok Creator Fund, creators will be able to realise additional earnings that help reward the care and dedication they put into creatively connecting with an audience that's inspired by their ideas.

To be eligible, users must be 18 years or older, meet a baseline for followers, and consistently post original content in line with our Community Guidelines. In a relatively short time, TikTok has grown to become a source of income and opportunity for creators and their families."

Source/More details: https://newsroom.tiktok.com/en-gb/tiktok-creator-fund-your-questions-answered

DIGI-PRENEUR

PROFILE - 5

Varalika Mishra
Founder, Your Story Is Important

Your Story Is Important
A social media initiative on mental and emotional health
It acts as a bridge to connect people who seek professional help with regard
to mental health.

Instagram: Your Story Is Important
Facebook: Your Story Is Important

Varalika founded *Your Story Is Important*-a leading online initiative on mental health in December 2019. She uses her channel to conduct dialogues & conversations with people who have experienced mental health issues and who work closely for this cause. Through social media, she acts as a bridge to connect people who are seeking professional help with regard to mental health.

"My work provides people a safe space to understand mental health and seek help from a professional. Through my initiative, I have collaborated with psychologists, therapists and psychiatrists so that people can easily approach me to seek help and get connected to a professional which is also a challenge for many people. My purpose is to be a catalyst in getting people's attention on the subject of mental health and social media helps me reach out to people from all walks of life no matter where they are," she says.

Some of the topics she focuses on include body shaming and its impact on mental health; dark skin is beautiful; men can have depression too; mental health of Kashmiri women and children; addiction and its impact on mental health; dance and its relationship with mental well-being; grief of losing a dog; dialogue on emotions and its impact on mental well-being; myths around mental health; mental health of women; music and its impact on mental health and many others.

As part of her initiative, she has held dialogues with Vijay Lokapally - Former Deputy Editor of Hindu on his own journey of depression and with Lalitha Kumaramangalam on women and their mental health with regard to sex workers and acid attack survivors. She also had a dialogue with Tania Singh who works closely with acid attack survivors. The main purpose of Your Story Is Important is to normalise the notion around mental health and break the stigma.

Varalika's initiative was covered prominently by many publications and platforms.

17

VLOGGING vs BLOGGING
WHICH IS BETTER?

As far as earning potential is concerned, both blogs and vlogs have their own dedicated niche.

A question that comes up very often among digital marketeers and content creators is whether it's better to vlog or blog. Let's find out.

Both blogging and vlogging involve creating content and the good news is that both of them hold great earning potential if you know how to optimise them properly. Blog refers to a short piece of written text about a specific topic-say, health, personal finance, travel or fitness, to name a few. They can be used to create awareness about products and services, and to also promote brands and businesses. A vlog comprises video content that serves the same purpose, and tells a story with accompanying visuals. So, instead of a written text about the importance of staying fit, a vlogger would talk about it with the help of videos. Both blogs and vlogs are equally effective, but if you're wondering which is the best option to get started, think first, about the amount of time commitment that is required for both vlogs and blogs vis-à-vis the time you have at hand.

Vlogging will take up much more of your time since its video-based and will require your complete involvement. Right from conceptualisation, to execution, to editing, it will demand most of your time and commitment. Blogging, on the other hand, is a lot less demanding. That's not to say that blogging isn't creative-it's just that the planning, implementation and editing processes are a lot simpler. The entire blogging process can be done by you-planning the content, writing and uploading it, and even editing/proof-reading it, but vlogs will need the help of extra hands-we'll see how, later.

As far as earning potential is concerned, both blogs and vlogs have their own dedicated niche. Some of the popular blogging platforms include WordPress, Blogger, Tumblr and Wix, while YouTube, Vimeo, Facebook and Dailymotion have earned their spot in the list of top vlogging sites till date.

BLOGGING

The one major skill you need to have for blogging is to be able to write impeccably. No grammatical errors, no spelling or punctuation gaffes-remember, blogs, with their combination of visual and text, must be able to make an impact even on the casual reader.

While writing, remember to keep it simple and straightforward. Your content must resonate with readers of every level, so make sure the words hit home. Appeal to the emotions-even the most technical piece of information can be explained in the simplest and most direct of ways. Conclude with the faintest of hints that there's more to come-the trick is to keep the readers hooked.

Remember to keep updating your blog posts. Especially if your aim is to attract more people to your brand, it makes absolute sense to keep up a sense of continuity. Find out different aspects about your business that will interest people. Enjoy the process of writing. Seek feedback. Get a second person to edit the blogs, if possible. Explore the possibility of getting guest writers or experts on a particular topic, to write about it. Stick to around 500 words-any more will distract the reader.

CONSIDER THE FOLLOWING BLOG POST EXTRACT:

Pathways English Academy is here to help you master the nuances of the English language. English is the most widely spoken language in the world, so wherever you go, you'll find you need English to get by. So, wouldn't you like to be a master in the language? Wouldn't you like to impress others with your impeccable English language skills? If your answer is "yes," then get in touch with us. We promise you you won't be disappointed! Now consider this:

Imagine walking into a room full of business delegates from different parts of the world. You're about to make a presentation to let them know why they must invest in your business. But words fail you-you get a niggling feeling deep down that you may not be able to express yourself clearly. You doubt your English language communication skills-you realise your ability to hold your own in the language is feeble. You're forced to excuse yourself and make an ignominious exit, your grand business plans down the drain.

Is this a situation you'd like to find yourself in? Or ever faced? If so, wouldn't you like to turn things around? To speak English like a dream, to cast a spell on everyone with your verbal prowess, to impress and to make a difference? to see your business prospects materialise and take shape? Oh, wouldn't you like to savour the flavour of success?

If you do, reach out to us at Pathways English Academy and feel the difference! Get ready to take on the world.
Which one do you think will make the greater impact? Why? If I said option 2, would you agree?

VLOGGING

Vlog just means Video Blog or a Video Log, and it refers to a blog that is completely visual-oriented. A vlog is often considered the most impactful way to reach your message across to your audience. What this means is that you create your own little TV show or channel where you build up a fan base and publish videos regularly that tell your story. If you can find the time for it, and invest in a good video editing software, then this is the best way to give your business that extra push. Like blogs, vlogs can be both personal and business focused. Some of the popular subjects for personal blogs are food, travel, technology, beauty, gaming, fitness, comedy, health & wellness and auto. Business blogs focus on products or service(s), but they often use the personal angle to drive home the message.

So, what's the difference between a YouTuber and a vlogger, you might ask? Well, a YouTuber publishes videos only on YouTube, while a vlogger publishes videos across multiple channels such as Facebook or Vimeo, to name a few. Is it more impactful to be a YouTuber or a vlogger? There's no clear answer here, it all depends on the content you create and the kind of audience you target.

Once you identify a platform (YouTube, Facebook etc,.) you'll need to decide what content to create, write a script for this content so that while filming you know the order in which everything happens, shoot the video and then edit it. Keep in mind that vlogging is not something you can do alone by yourself. You'll need people to help-someone to shoot the video (especially if it's outdoors), co-stars with you in the vlog unless you decide to be the only one on camera, and finally someone to edit the whole footage. Unless you're a professional editor and photographer all rolled into one, you'll most definitely need someone to trim all unwanted portions from your video, add music and other special effects for that extra hit and input text with your contact details (if you're promoting your brand), so that your final output is clean, seamless and professional.

Any content creator with experience will tell you that a mix of blogging and vlogging is actually much more impactful than just one of these mediums-especially for brand/business promotion. Maintain a consistent blog with links to your vlog sites and vice-versa. Keep your audience hooked both ways. Do this, and you'll see how powerful the digital world can be.

18

PODCASTS-IN OR OUT?

The convenience of podcasts makes consumers listen to an entire episode in one go, which makes it a great medium for businesses to cultivate brand loyalty and a dedicated listener base.

Known as 'Radio-on-Demand,' podcasts are pre-recorded audio programmes that can be accessed online through a subscription, or downloaded onto a device to play back later.

Podcasts are a form of online audio broadcast (although some video podcasts are available today) and they have become a mainstream content source: people consume it just as they would a video or a TV series. With the mobile user base growing more than ever, podcasts have become a sure-fire way of reaching out to audiences of all demographies-an invaluable content marketing tool. In fact, so popular are they, that they are in direct contention with videos as a platform for brand promotion and marketing.

In the past, podcasts were confined to iPods, computers or media players on phones. Today, however, advancements in hand held devices, laptops and bluetooth speakers have catapulted podcasts onto the hotseat, with the education sector increasingly relying on it for the easy and effortless transmission of information.

However, small business owners often find it confusing to decide between podcasts and videos as a content marketing and distribution medium. In a scenario where investing in digital infrastructure still comes with a "luxury" budget tag, many small entrepreneurs wonder whether to put their money on the visual or the audio medium. Is it better to start a YouTube channel today, or can I reach my target audience better through a series of podcasts?

THE PROS

Podcasts are usually accessed via as an app and feature as a series of episodes that can be downloaded onto your phone or laptop to listen to whenever convenient-at the gym, while driving, or even while you cook. As opposed to this, a video mandates both your visual and auditory senses to function simultaneously in order to capture the entire experience-this requires you to be seated and in complete attention to the screen, and multitasking is often not possible. Experts say the convenience of podcasts makes consumers listen to an entire episode in one go, which makes it a great medium for businesses to cultivate brand loyalty and a dedicated listener base.

Each podcast revolves around a certain theme that appears as episodes. So they're ideal for small business that focus on delivering a particular product or service. For instance, if you're a small entrepreneur with a business that specialises in health and wellness products, your business could create a podcast on health-related topics and use that to promote your products. With its 'audio-on-demand' tag that allows customers to access YOUR message on THEIR terms, podcasts are a great way to get your brand noticed.

Then again, podcasts require little or no infrastructure to get started-just perhaps a hand-held mic and a smartphone with a good quality voice recorder. This makes it ideal for small entrepreneurs who're not yet comfortable being seen on screen.

THE CONS

Podcasts are one-sided and offers only audio, while video is considered the more "complete experience." With its striking visuals and impactful music, videos, especially those on You-Tube, remain the most preferred content creation platform to date. Podcasts are more impacted by distractions. Since it allows for multi-tasking, it is easy for listeners to tune out of a podcast if they are distracted by something else.

Podcasts require more time than videos to research, script and deliver. Because they are sound-focused, podcasts scripts must be simple and easy to understand, while being informative and engaging. This may prove arduous for small businesses that are short on time and the necessary resources to research and prepare regular podcast scripts.

Last, but not the least, podcasts require sound editing software-and extensive knowledge of sound mixing and editing.
So, the final choice is entirely up to you-consider your audience, your goals, your budget and the kind of product or service you are offering before making a decision. If you'd like to listen to a podcast before you decide, log on to Spotify, Google Podcasts or Apple Podcasts.

PODCAST MARKET

Podcasts are the fastest growing content creation medium-in fact, according to Podcast Insights 2021, there are over two million podcasts in the world today and the number is all set to grow. Here's another mind-blowing statistic: In 2020, the global podcast market was worth USD 11.46 billion and is expected to keep growing at a CAGR of 31.1% between 2021 and 2028. See where it's headed?

KPMG's Media and Entertainment Report 2020 found that India recorded a 29.3 % increase in podcast consumption in the first year of the pandemic. According to PwC's Global Entertainment & Media Outlook 2020 report, India is the third largest consumer of podcasts (after the US and China), with 57.6 million monthly listeners.

Sources:

- *https://www.podcastinsights.com/podcast-statistics*
- *KPMG Media and Entertainment Report, 2020*
- *PWC Global Entertainment and Media Outlook 2020-2024*

DIGI-PRENEUR

PROFILE - 6

Deepak Nair
Entrepreneur and Digital Media Pioneer

Deepak Nair
Founder, Editor & CEO
Interactive Digital Media Technologies LLC
www.interacoman.com
www.destinationoman.com
www.omanvistas.com
www.ktexplorer.com

https://www.linkedin.com/in/deepak-nair-25b0471

Deepak Nair is an accomplished IT & Media professional having over three decades of experience. He is the CEOcalled InteracOman (www.interacoman.com) in 1999.

A serial entrepreneur since then, as a tribute to his host country, Deepak also founded the first privately owned multiple award winning tourism portal in Oman called DestinationOman (www.destinationoman.com) in 2001 which also has an annual printed edition that is like a pictorial treatise capturing the natural beauty of Oman and its tourism destinations.

In 2006, Deepak founded the web portal *Oman Vistas*, www.omanvistas.com, where Omani companies get the opportunity to connect with their audiences digitally.

In 2017, wanting to do his bit for his home state of Kerala, which is called God's own country, Deepak founded Kerala Travel Explorer (www.ktexplorer.com) as a web portal and magazine to create better awareness of Kerala to the world outside. Deepak has been using social media to expand the reach and resonance of his company. In his words: *"Social media marketing is one key element of our business these days, social media marketing helps us to reach our targeted audience within a short span of time. Along with our online presence via websites, SMM channels get better online presence. Social media channels serves as a content distribution platform that can make proper use of the available digital tools and to grab maximum attention and reach. Another best use of social media marketing is that we can do competitor analysis easily. This information can include their ad and content promotion strategies. With that data we can make a comprehensive analysis to reap more benefits from ads and marketing in a unique way, by revising and upgrading our strategies. One key attraction of SMM is there are no geographical restrictions, we can target audiences from any corner of the world and therefore, we can expand our client base without any boundaries. Social media paid ads are another key element that helps us get enquiries and leads from our target audience. Through social media channels we can build a connection with our target audience and potential clients, we can offer better customer service also. From our experience , we would like to say that social media is vital for better branding, credibility, and customer loyalty if we implement it in the right way.*

Organic search is a critical component of most businesses website performance to get enquiries, leads and calls directly from the website. The key advantage of SEO is its cost effectiveness compared with other digital marketing strategies and SEO results are long-lasting if we do it properly. Establishing a brand as an authority takes patience, effort, and commitment and relies on offering a valuable, quality product or service that allows custom-

ers to trust a brand, so we rely on SEO as our Search Engine Marketing strategy.

We currently having social media marketing channels on Facebook, Instagram, Twitter and LinkedIn, and we implement Search Engine Marketing via SEO, out of all these we found the best as Facebook marketing & SEO, that gives us the best results and leads so far. As on social media each channel has a unique trait and is used for different purposes, not all social media channels are compatible with all business types. However, Facebook is one medium that goes well with almost every business type. Considering the search engine visibility ,SEO gives our brand the credibility and brand value, and it contributes actively towards expanding brand awareness.

Following are his ventures:

- **Interactive Digital Media Technologies LLC,** was founded in 1999 by foccuses on website development for corporate customers in the Sultanate of Oman.www.interacoman.com

  https://www.facebook.com/InteracOman
  https://www.instagram.com/interacoman/
  https://twitter.com/InteracOman
  www.linkedin.com/company/interacoman

- **DestinationOman**
  www.destinationoman.com
  Destination Oman is an online Oman travel directory dedicated towards Oman tourism

  https://www.facebook.com/DestinationsOman/
  https://www.linkedin.com/company/destinationoman
  https://www.instagram.com/destinationoman2/
  https://twitter.com/destinationoman

- **Oman Vistas**
  www.omanvistas.com

  Established in 2007 Oman Vistas is a Digital PR webportal.

  https://www.facebook.com/OmanVistas-165663050145308/
  https://www.linkedin.com/company/79882108/admin/
  https://twitter.com/omanvistas
  https://www.instagram.com/omanvistas/

19

OTT PLATFORMS: DRIVING THE CHANGE

OTT platforms are cost-effective and allow for the geograph-ical targeting of the audience, niche viewership and detailed measurement metrics.

OTT - *Over-The-Top* - platforms have been garnering sig-nificant attention and interest in the last few years. Think Netflix, Amazon Prime, Hulu, Apple +, Peacock or Disney Plus, to name a few. They've always been popular, but the Covid-19 pandemic only increased public appetite for OTT content. And as people rapidly switch from traditional media platforms to the digital ones, OTTs have caught the eye of content marketeers who realised the power of the platform as a powerful tool to reach out. Why is it such a popular medium? Because it brings the excitement of TV advertising combined with the precision of target marketing, which makes it an irresistible force. So, while the general public browses their favourite shows on Netflix, Disney or Amazon Prime, content marketeers look for customised, personalised ways to reach their audience and maximise their Return on Investment (ROI).

The explosive growth of OTT platforms make them a not-to-miss content marketing tool. Why? Because they are cost effective, allow for geographical targeting of the audience, niche viewership and detailed measurement metrics. Moreover, it is possible to drive powerful, data-driven campaigns on OTT platforms, making it the perfect marketing tool for businesses. Let's look at how OTT platforms allow precise targeting of potential customers. Each subscriber to a particular OTT platform is assigned a specific user ID. This information is used by content marketeers to understand audience preferences and provide personalised ads that will interest users.

Let's say, for instance, that you own a business dealing in health and wellness products for the 18-35 age group. OTT platforms, will help you identify users within that age group that are keen on health and wellness.

Again, contrary to popular perception, OTT platforms do actually allow for enhanced viewer measurement and metrics. OTT platforms have stringent regulations that prevent third party apps from interfering with the viewing experience. Content marketeers can tap into this scenario by collaborating with publishers to produce ads that are unintrusive and do not disrupt the viewing experience.

Now comes the most important part: OTT platforms facilitate better ROI. This is because the OTT audience is smaller (since they are paid for), and so facilitate better reach and engagement. There's also the advantage of localisation. With more and more people spanning languages and cultures becoming familiar with OTT platforms, shows and movies have become available in multiple languages, which in turn have resulted in higher retention rates.

However, OTT platforms have been facing a few challenges, especially since the onset of the pandemic. They depend on an ever-increasing addition to their library of shows and movies for their popularity and so the pandemic-induced restrictions slowed their momentum, as there were very few new items to add to their collection. Also, since the competition in this space is stiff, OTT platforms felt they would lose out if users realised that their preferences were not being prioritised. So they relied on AI & analytics to make their interface more user-friendly and intuitive.

20

CONTENT CREATION ON OTT PLATFORMS

Identify one unique aspect that will set aside your content from competition-why would your audience want to view your content over someone else's?

There's no doubt that OTT and streaming platforms are growing at breakneck speed. So, content strategy & creation for these platforms require much thought and vision. Remember, people preferences and technologies change and so be prepared to keep fine-tuning your strategy to keep pace with the changes.

As always, keep the audience at the centre of your content strategy. What devices do they like to watch the videos on? Are you targeting a specific demographic? What kind of content do they like to see?

Whatever they want is what you give-just make sure your message isn't lost in the process. Your content strategy must reflect the vision and mission of your brand-whatever you create must integrate this vision into it. Identify one unique aspect that will set aside your content from competition-why would your audience want to view your content over someone else's? Will your content be a specialised genre, or will it span/combine a series of genres?

Again, what does your strategy hope to achieve? Some of the most popular and obvious choices include more money, more reach, a loyal customer base and viewer engagement. Is there anything else you would like to achieve with your strategy? Identify as many goals as possible, since these will add clarity to your planning. Also figure out how lengthy you'd like your content to be-will it be something you'd like your viewers to binge on over the weekend? Or is it something you'd like them to watch everyday for a few minutes during their daily office commute? These are just the tip of the iceberg-content strategy, creation, monetising and distribution across OTT platform deserves a separate book altogether, as well as specialised marketing skills.

21

ANALYSING CONTENT

*Content analytics provides valuable insights about
how your audience behave while they consume
your content.*

So, you've strategised, created and distributed your content. But don't you want to know whether it's doing its job of promoting your brand? Is there any part of it that isn't working? Is there anything that needs to be played up? Critical insights that will make or break your business, going forward. This is where content analytics steps in.

Remember, it's not just enough to create and market your content-you must analyse it thoroughly if it is to make the desired impact. Analysing the way your content is consumed is a must for effective marketing campaigns and better business outcomes. Content analytics provides valuable insights about how your audience behave while they consume your content. Here's what content analysis helps you achieve:

1.   Getting to know your audience-We know now how crucial it is know your audience, if your content creation and marketing strategies are to work. An effective content analysis tool will classify your audience by age, gender, demography, location, interests, etc. It will also tell you the device, the browser and operating system with which your users have accessed your content. This not only lets you create content specific to demographic type, but it also helps you ensure that your website or channel is compatible with these technologies, so that the user experience is enhanced.

2.   Content analytic tools also help you understand what kind of content performs best, so that you can create more such types for maximum impact. More importantly, you can also stop wasting time on what doesn't work.

3.   Analytics helps you with your SEO goals-and this, we know, is what drives digital content and boosts your business performance. It allows you to monitor the performance of your keywords, so that you can figure out how much traffic each word brings.

4.   Advanced analytics tools also help you identify what exactly your site visitors are looking for when they visit your website/channel. This allows you to find out whether your content meets user expectations. Plus, it gives you topic ideas for your next blog or video.

Most content creators fail to utilise the full potential of a content analytics tool because of which they fail to maximise the effectiveness of their content. Many digital marketers believe that not having a content analytics does not necessarily hurt your SEO rankings. However, if you're a business organisation or an entrepreneur that's just starting out, it is highly recommended that you invest in a strong analytics tool to boost your visibility and ranking in the digital realm.

DIGI-PRENEUR

PROFILE - 7

Harpreet Ahluwalia
Founder & CEO, Earthly Creations

"Love an animal, gift a plant, now and always."
Making lives beautiful through gardening ,
Earthly Creations specialises in all kinds of hand-made
garden decor & garden accessories.

https://earthlycreations.in/
https://www.youtube.com/channel/UCJwFJebTD970G-xr5blqL0Q/
https://www.instagram.com/earthlycreations_ec/LinkedIn- https://
www.linkedin.com/in/harpreet-ahluwalia-0b59a25/
https://www.facebook.com/search/top?q=earthlycreations

Harpreet's Earthly Creations is a socio-economic venture that equips artists with opportunities to generate sustainable employment. Earthly Creations works with potters and rural artisans to enrich their lives, since being in the informal sector makes them vulnerable to many challenges. "*According to an estimate, there are over four million potters in India who operate and manufacture products on conventional pottery wheels. Of these, a vast majority are involved in making traditional and conventional red local pottery for the local market*".

"Pottery is primarily a village industry and operates in an informal setting with rudimentary technology, organisation and marketing network," Harpreet says. *"They produce for the village and regions where they live and do not go beyond its limits. The pots and items that they manufacture are often sold only in the local village markets and nowhere else,"* she adds.

Having a digital presence and marketing products digitally become important when connecting with markets, communities and customers. *"We've adopted a strategic approach to reach out through social media platforms and digital commerce platforms. This, in turn, helps us enhance the potter artisans' income and welfare,"* Harpreet points out.

"We, at Earthly Creations, contemporise designs to suit today's needs. We've also inspired the artisans families to invest in their daughters' education by providing them with scholarships, thereby preventing social ills such as child marriages and teenage pregnancies. We also facilitate interventions on women empowerment and impart management skills to budding entrepreneurs. Not only that, we also help corporates and individuals curate green gifts made by potters across India. We also provide 1:1 consulting services and hold workshops on various gardening topics such as turning kitchen waste into food, growing microgreens and balcony gardening," she adds.

22

CAN TRADITIONAL CONTENT CREATION METHODS SURVIVE?

The idea is that the traditional-modern approach to content strategy and marketing is much more powerful than a 'traditional-only' or 'digital-only' approach.

The simple answer is YES. It can, provided it is created to fit in with digital trends. In this sense, traditional media (read PRINT) is not dead-it just has to prove itself worthy of standing up to its digital counterpart.

The first step for traditional media is to completely overhaul its processes-print content strategy was limited, at best, to a flatplan for a particular publication. The focus of the publication remained unchanged; it was a take-it-or-leave-it situation. Now, with digital content, the strategy needs to be customer-first and build for the future by integrating the lessons of the past. So, if you're a traditional content generation source, be ready to invest time and resources towards a robust, customer-first content strategy and plan.

The second step is to invest in a digital platform and digital marketing techniques that help promote your traditional, long form content. Then, using the analytics from that platform to create content that would interest the most loyal demographic visitors to the platform. This helps build a stronger rapport with your existing and potential customers by giving them the kind of content they would like to read. Investing in digital marketing techniques will also provide you with alternative revenue models and allow to combine ad-supported and paid content formats.

Apps and websites are another way to drive traffic to your traditional content source. Create an app or a website that provides snippets of the traditional content you have on offer. You could initially keep it free to use and eventually charge a nominal subscription fee.

You could make these digital tools interactive by adding videos, providing content sharing and tagging options and comparison links that compare your content or product with that of another. Create online communities that bring together your customers for better interaction and feedback. Go social. Focus on videos.

The idea is that the traditional-modern approach to content strategy and marketing is much more powerful than a 'traditional-only' or 'digital-only' approach. As long as you're willing to experiment and focus on your target audience, this hybrid approach is not a bad thing.

23

CAN I USE CONTENT TO MAKE MONEY ONLINE?

The only limit is your imagination, so there's really no stopping you if you're clear about what you want and how you want it.

Perhaps the most frequently asked question anywhere today: is it possible for me to make money online with my content?Before we get into the details, let it be known that it may not ALWAYS be possible to make money online. Reason: stiff competition and a fast-evolving content landscape. However, there are some tried and tested ways to make your content shine, so that it is easy for the money to flow in.

One of them is blogging. We've seen how to create content on blogs, but how do you optimise blogs to make them effective money-attracting channels?

Blogging isn't perhaps the easiest way to make money, but that's not to say you can't. To begin with, you have two options when considering a blog for your business-the free blogging sites and the paid ones. The free sites are easy to set up, but come with storage limits, so you can't upload too many videos or customise templates/themes. Neither can you run too many banner ads or affiliate marketing links which are the chief sources of revenue from blogs. Then again, the URL for your blog will contain the name of the blogging site and not an exclusive name that you would like. For instance, www.brilliantstars.blogspot.com, as opposed to brilliantstarsgiftstore.com. So, if your aim is just a casual blog site for your writing pleasure, then these sites are the way to go. If, however, your aim is to generate content to make your brand shine, then you must consider the paid sites. In fact, most blogging platforms have free and paid versions.

The best way to make money from blogs is to use the paid platforms to create your own website. It may seem daunting, but this seriously is the best way to go. You will have complete control over key aspects like design and customisation, and you can run as many ads or affiliate marketing links as you like. This is where you can give free rein to your content and be as imaginative and as creative as you like. Just remember to supplement your text with visuals and/or videos, for that extra impact. These blog sites will be your personal brand identity and give you total control. Another way to blog is to write for corporates or brands. In the vast digital ecosystem, it is possible to bid for these corporate writing projects either by being directly employed with a corporate firm, or by bidding for them on gig platforms such as Fiverr, Upwork, Guru, Flexjobs and many more. All you need to do is create a profile and search for short-duration freelance jobs that fit your requirement(s).

Once you've created your content, it's time to bring in the audience. So promote your blog on social media-in fact, set up dedicated Facebook and Instagram pages for your blog site and keep giving your followers a sneak preview of what's next in your blog. Invest in paid ads to increase traction, and keep posting regularly. Also make sure to connect with other bloggers-this increases visibility and bloggers often promote each other, even if they're competition.

Now let's look at vlogging.

Although vlogs are becoming increasingly popular, there's no quick and easy mantra to start earning money. You'll have to sweat it out, be consistent and have lots of patience. Remember, not all vloggers make money, so you'll have to stand out exceptionally well if you must. The first thing to keep in mind is that the content of your video is important-so it is imperative that you take time to identify a niche that you'd like to be known for. Of course, if you're looking at business promotion, then choosing a content becomes easier-you'll focus on the product or the service that you're offering. Give yourself enough time to plan your content-how you treat content is as important as what the content is. Make sure that each video you publish treats content in a unique, interesting way.

Video promotions are the most important advertising trend that no content marketeer can afford to miss. The interesting thing is that video promos can be part of your vlog-the initial few seconds, in fact.

Video promotions are simple: when you make your video, make sure that the first few seconds count. The beginning is always important, since that sets the tone for what is about to come. The visuals must be arresting, as well as the audio. Put yourself in your customers' shoes. Ask yourself why someone must prefer your brand over the others in the market. And decide to tell them exactly why, in your video. Similarly, why must someone watch my video (if it's a personal one)? Tell them why.

Digital publishing: Publishing is big business, it has always been. What has changed between now and then is in the manner in which it's done. Whereas the publishing process back then involved a lengthy concatenation of author-agent-editor and publisher, today, this has shifted to the digital realm, where the owner is the author, editor and publisher all at once. This means that if you decide to write a book today, you can do so with great joy: gone is the painful wait to hear from the publisher (followed by a rejection), and if accepted, the reworking of your content as per their instructions. The long timeline of frustrating delays are completely done away with and you can write your book and upload it on on-the many demand digital publishing platforms like Amazon (KDP) and LuluxPress, to name a few. With each sale of the book, you get a share in the royalty. Of course, you'll need to design a good cover and frame it as per the platform specifications before you upload.

These are just some of the many different ways to get your content to work, but bottom line is all about creativity. Creating content requires great skill and attention to detail. The only limit is your imagination, so there's really no stopping you, if you're clear about what you want and how you want it.

24

DISPELLING SOME MYTHS

If ever you're faced with a choice between writing top-notch content and taking a break between posting content to plan and strategise, opt for the latter. Quality shows, quality speaks.

Like everything else, digital content is also shrouded in myths and misunderstandings. It wouldn't be sensible to conclude this journey of discovery without dispelling some of them. So, here we go:

MYTH 1

#CONTENT WRITING=BLOGS

REALITY: NO. Blogs are just ONE WAY of creating content. As we have seen, there are other forms of content, like vlogs and podcasts, to name a few.

MYTH 2

#DIGITAL CONTENT=INCREASED COSTS

REALITY: NO. If you know what the purpose of your content is, you'll find that the investments you make towards digital content are significantly less than your traditional content investments.

MYTH 3

#DIGITAL CONTENT CREATORS=TECHNOLOGY WIZARDS

REALITY: NO. Digital content creators are not experts. They just know what tool must be used where, to maximise content value and reach. The entire process of content creation is a team effort-experts in one area supplement the experts in another, to produce output that sells.

MYTH 4

#DIGITAL CONTENT=QUANTITY OVER QUALITY

REALITY: NO. Although consistency is key, quality is absolutely paramount. If ever you're faced with a choice between writing top-notch content and taking a break between posting content to plan and strategise, opt for the latter. Quality shows, quality speaks.

MYTH 5
#DIGITAL CONTENT=KEYWORD DENSITY

REALITY: NO. Keywords drive SEO, they're important to rank high on search, but that's not the be-all and end-all of digital content. If you've produced something that speaks directly to the audience, appeals to their emotions and makes them want to reach out to you, then you've done it-keyword or not.

25

TO SUM IT ALL UP...

Despite your best-laid plans, your content can fail. It may not bring in the cash you wish, it may not create a loyal fan following and it may not even be received well.

The digital content world is vast, fast-evolving and yet to be completely understood. There's plenty of potential in this area if you know how to tap into it and unleash its powers. Creating digital content is not easy, however, it need not be a futile endeavour if you have a proper strategy and distribution plan in place. Businesses that plan to grow and thrive MUST invest in digital content creation essentials, the most important of which is a skilled and experienced team.

One of the first rules for any content creator is to always keep his audience in mind because without knowing who you're creating content for and what it is that they want, all attempts at content creation are doomed to fail. So first and foremost, identify and understand your target audience. Then create a strategy to woo them with your content. Figure out how this content will be distributed. Use analytics to know how your content is faring. Get as much feedback from your customers as possible.

A word of caution here: despite your *best-laid* plans, your content can fail. It may not bring in the cash you wish, it may not create a loyal fan following and it may even not be received well. Remember, digital content is rapidly changing and its paradigms constantly shifting even as you read this.

So make sure every step you take is carefully thought out and in tune with market demands. What may be in vogue today may be trashed tomorrow, so keep your finger on the pulse. Be ready to constantly adapt, change, innovate and invent. There's an exciting virtual world out there for the fearless, so get ready to welcome it with open arms.

REFERENCES

Appel, G., Grewal, L., Hadi, R. et al(2020). The future of social media in marketing. J. of the Acad. Mark. Sci. 48, 79–95). https://doi.org/10.1007/s11747-019-00695-1

Content Marketing Institute, What Is Content Marketing? <http://contentmarketinginstitute.com/what-is-content-marketing/

Content Marketing Institute. (2017). Why is Content Marketing Today's Marketing? 10 Stats That Prove It. [online] Available at: <http://contentmarketinginstitute.com/2016/08/content-marketing-stats/

Demand Metric, A Guide to Marketing Genius: Content Marketing,   https://www.demandmetric.com/content/content-marketing-infographic

Darius Daniel (2020), The Impact of Social Media Adoption by Companies. Digital Transformation,Sciendo,   https://doi.org/10.2478/sues-2020-0014

Forrest PJ, Content Marketing Today, https://www.researchgate.net/publication/331345065_Content_Marketing_Today

Martin Labbé (2009) How to Market Music from Developing Countries Online, WIPO

Nolan, H. (2018), Brands are creating virtual influencers, Which could make the Kardashians a thing of the past, https://tinyurl.com/y7gu7t26.

Nill, A., & Aalberts, R. J. (2014). Legal and ethical challenges of online behavioral targeting in advertising. Journal of Current Issues and Research in Advertising, 35, 126–146.

Oxford Economics, The state of the creator economy, Oxford Economics Research Report on Creator Economy https://resources.oxfordeconomics.com/hubfs/YouTube_US_The_state_of_the_creator_economy.pdf

Oxford Economics, From opportunity to impact assessing the economic, societal, and cultural benefits of YouTube in Canada, https://www.oxfordeconomics.com/recent-releases/From-Opportunity-to-Impact-Assessing-the-Economic-Societal-and-Cultural-Benefits-of-YouTube-in-Canada

Pennycook, G., Cannon, T. D., & Rand, D. G. (2019). Prior exposure increases perceived accuracy of fake news. Journal of Experimental Psychology: General In press.

Safko, L. (2010). The social media bible: Tactics, tools, and strategies for business success. John Wiley & Sons.

TikTok Creator Fund: Your questions answered <https://newsroom.tiktok.com/en-gb/tiktok-creator-fund-your-ques-

tions-answered>

UNIDO, Branding for Competitiveness and Sustainable Growth https://www.unido.org/b4c

UNCTAD (2021) The Digital Economy Report 2021, https://unctad.org/system/files/official-document/der2021_en.pdf

Villarroel Ordenes, F., Ludwig, S., De Ruyter, K., Grewal, D., & Wetzels, M. (2017). Unveiling what is written in the stars: Analyzing explicit, implicit, and discourse patterns of sentiment in social media. Journal of Consumer Research, 43(6), 875–894.

WIPO/ICT (2003) Marketing Crafts and Visual Arts:The Role of Intellectual Property,https://www.wipo.int/edocs/pubdocs/en/intproperty/itc_p159/wipo_pub_itc_p159.pdf